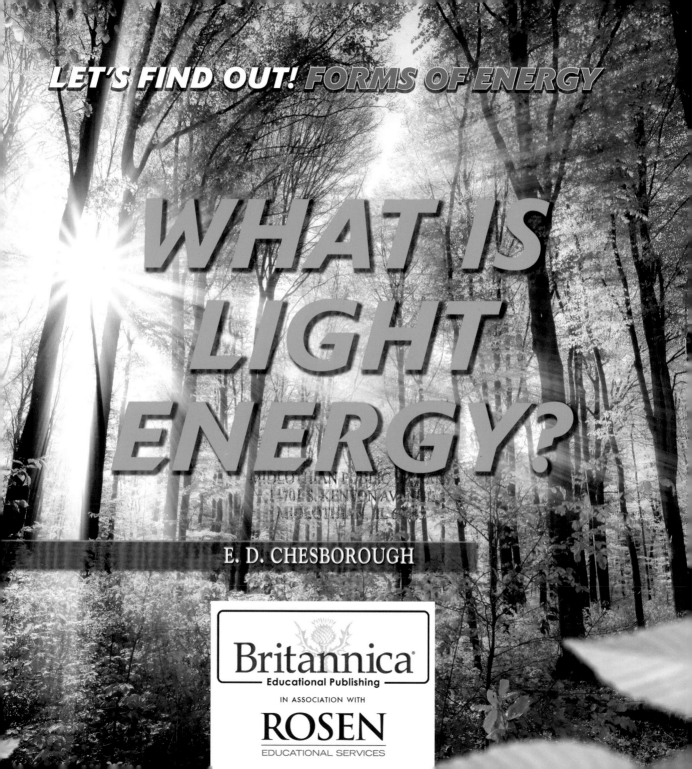

WHAT IS LIGHT ENERGY?

E. D. CHESBOROUGH

Britannica
Educational Publishing

IN ASSOCIATION WITH

ROSEN
EDUCATIONAL SERVICES

Published in 2018 by Britannica Educational Publishing (a trademark of Encyclopædia Britannica, Inc.) in association with The Rosen Publishing Group, Inc.
29 East 21st Street, New York, NY 10010

Distributed exclusively by Rosen Publishing.
To see additional Britannica Educational Publishing titles, go to rosenpublishing.com.

First Edition

Britannica Educational Publishing
J.E. Luebering: Executive Director, Core Editorial
Mary Rose McCudden: Editor, Britannica Student Encyclopedia

Rosen Publishing
Amelie von Zumbusch: Editor
Nelson Sá: Art Director
Nicole Russo-Duca: Designer
Cindy Reiman: Photography Manager
Karen Huang: Photo Researcher

Library of Congress Cataloging-in-Publication Data

Names: Chesborough, E. D., author.
Title: What is light energy? / E.D. Chesborough.
Description: First edition. | New York, NY : Britannica Educational Publishing in association with Rosen Educational Services, 2018. | Series: Let's find out! Forms of energy | Includes bibliographical references and index. | Audience: 1-4.
Identifiers: LCCN 2016058553 | ISBN 9781680487077 (library bound ; alk. paper) | ISBN 9781680487053 (pbk.; alk. paper) | ISBN 9781680487060 (6-pack ; alk. paper)
Subjects: LCSH: Light—Juvenile literature.
Classification: LCC QC360 .C53 2018 | DDC 535—dc23
LC record available at https://lccn.loc.gov/2016058553

Manufactured in the United States of America

Photo credits: Cover, p. 1 Smileus/Shutterstock.com; p. 4 Alena Ozerova/Shutterstock.com; p. 5 Paper Cat/Shutterstock.com; p. 6 oliveromg/Shutterstock.com; p. 7 hxdbzxy/Shutterstock.com; p. 8 Rebroad; p. 9 Anita P Peppers/Fotolia; p. 10 Roxana Bashyrova /Shutterstock.com; p. 11 Steve Mann/Shutterstock.com; pp. 12, 16, 20, 24 Encyclopædia Britannica, Inc.; p. 13 Polonez/Shutterstock .com; p. 14 John and Penny/Shutterstock.com; p. 15 © Merriam-Webster Inc.; p. 17 Samantha Roche/Fotolia; p. 18 Imagentle /Shutterstock.com; p. 19 NASA; p. 21 Mark Herreid/Shutterstock.com; p. 22 Mike Harrington/Digital Vision/Getty Images; p. 23 Copyright © 1971 Z. Leszczynski/Animals Animals; p. 25 Bokeh Blur Background Subject/Shutterstock.com; p. 26 © Matthew Bowden/ Fotolia; p. 27 © Vibe Images/Fotolia; p. 28 Nalle_och_SFO/E+/Getty Images; p. 29 Michael Photo/Shutterstock.com; interior pages background image wenani/Shutterstock.com.

CONTENTS

EVERYTHING LIGHT TOUCHES

People and other animals need light in order to see. Look around you. Everything you see is illuminated by a source of light! Light is a form of energy. Living things need energy to move, work, and grow.

During the day, most of our light comes from the sun. Without the energy from

To reach Earth, light from the sun travels about 93 million miles (150 million kilometers).

Today, people use electricity to produce light. At night, cities like New York glow with electric light.

the sun, there would be no plants or animals on Earth's surface. Before humans learned to harness light on their own, nearly all light energy found on Earth came from the sun. Eventually, humans learned to build fires and then to use electricity. This ability to control our environment was a huge step forward for humankind.

Energy fuels our universe, from the stars in the sky to the tiniest algae in the sea. Light energy that began its journey out in space allows us to grow our food, light our homes, and do much more.

FORMS OF ENERGY

While light is one form of energy, it is not the only one. We can feel heat energy given off by fire. We hear noises thanks to sound energy. All of the foods we eat have chemical energy stored in them. Mechanical energy is the energy that a moving object—such as a ball that you kicked—has because of its movement and position. Electrical energy is associated with the flow of tiny particles

The chemical energy stored in a person's muscles can be transformed into the mechanical energy needed to pedal a bike.

Cars transform the chemical energy stored in gasoline. What other things run on gasoline?

called electrons between atoms. Atoms are the tiny units that make up everything in the universe.

Energy can be transformed, or changed, from one form to another. Lightbulbs let us transform electrical energy to light energy. Chemical energy from burning gasoline transforms into mechanical energy that powers our cars and trucks. The electrical energy from a lightning bolt can strike the ground and give off heat energy.

THINK ABOUT IT

What are some examples of different forms of energy that you have noticed around you?

SOURCES OF LIGHT

Besides the sun, other sources provide light. Fire and burning objects give off light and heat. For example, torches, candles, and oil lamps are all sources of light. When they burn, a chemical reaction occurs that releases the energy we see as light. These were humans' first sources of light after sunlight.

Lightning is another natural source of light. Lightning is a form of electricity that is released from Earth's atmosphere during

When candles burn, a chemical reaction takes place that releases light energy.

Fireflies have special body parts that make light by mixing chemicals with oxygen from the air.

thunderstorms. Humans learned to produce electrical energy using chemical, mechanical, and nuclear energy. Now electrical energy is used to power lightbulbs.

Some animals, such as fireflies and certain fish, can give off light. Plants and animals that glow in the dark—glowworms, fireflies, and some mushrooms—change the chemical energy stored in their tissues to light energy.

Vocabulary

Nuclear energy is the energy that holds together the nucleus, or center, of an atom. Pulling apart a nucleus, or squishing together two nuclei, produces a lot of energy.

Properties of Light

Light exists in two different forms at the same time. One form is tiny particles called photons. The other form of light is waves. The easiest way to think about light is as waves, like those in the ocean. Light waves travel through space at extremely fast speeds.

Scientists use an idea called wavelength to describe light waves. Like waves moving across a pool of water, light waves have peaks and valleys. The distance between two of these high or low points is

The light from the stars you can see in the night sky has traveled vast distances to reach Earth.

Think About It

Can you imagine how fast light travels? Light waves travel through space at a speed of about 186,282 miles (299,792 kilometers) per second.

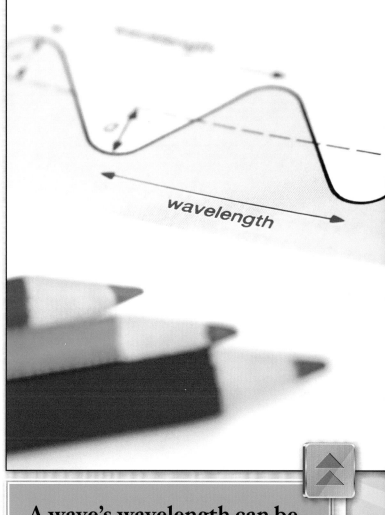

wavelength

called a wavelength. The sunlight we see each day contains light waves with long, medium, and short wavelengths. We see light of some wavelengths, but not all, with our eyes. To see other wavelengths, we need special tools.

A wave's wavelength can be measured from one peak to the next peak, or from one valley to the next valley.

UNDERSTANDING RADIATION

Radiation is energy that moves from place to place. Light, sound, and heat are all examples of radiation. The two main categories of radiation are electromagnetic and mechanical.

Light is electromagnetic radiation. Electromagnetic radiation comes from atoms, the building blocks of all matter. Some of the particles that make up atoms have

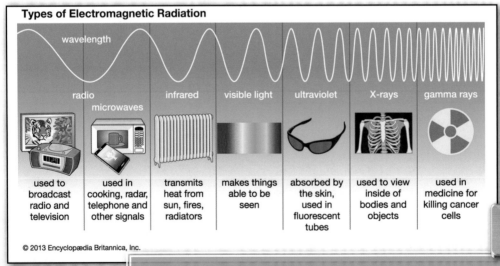

Types of Electromagnetic Radiation

wavelength

radio microwaves	infrared	visible light	ultraviolet	X-rays	gamma rays
used to broadcast radio and television	used in cooking, radar, telephone and other signals	transmits heat from sun, fires, radiators	makes things able to be seen	absorbed by the skin, used in fluorescent tubes	used to view inside of bodies and objects	used in medicine for killing cancer cells

© 2013 Encyclopædia Britannica, Inc.

Different kinds of electromagnetic radiation have different wavelengths.

an electric charge. The motion of these charged particles produces energy that can be described as traveling as waves. These waves can travel through empty space, like in outer space. They can also travel through air and even solid substances, such as glass.

Mechanical radiation cannot travel through empty space. It can only travel through a substance, such as air, water, or a solid object. One example of mechanical radiation is sound energy. An earthquake produces another type of mechanical radiation. The shock waves created by an earthquake travel through Earth and cause the ground to shake.

Light travels faster than sound, so you see lightning before you hear thunder.

COMPARE AND CONTRAST
How are mechanical radiation and electromagnetic radiation similar? How are they different?

LIGHT AND COLOR

Without light, there is no color. When people see colors, they are really seeing different types of light bouncing off objects.

The color of light depends on its wavelength. Each color has its own wavelength. Red light has the longest wavelength. Violet light has the shortest wavelength. Orange, yellow, green, blue, and indigo have wavelengths in between those of red and violet. When light waves of all the colors travel together, the light looks white. The range of colors is called the **visible spectrum**. It consists of all the colors we see around us. The

We see the different wavelengths of light that bounce off this fruit as color.

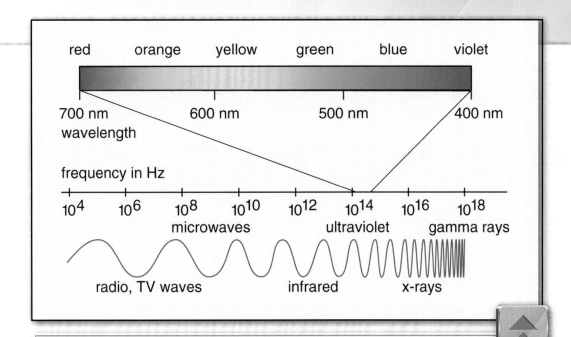

Only a small portion of the electromagnetic spectrum is visible to the human eye.

visible spectrum is a small part of the total range, or spectrum, of all electromagnetic radiation. Other kinds of radiation, including X-rays and radio waves, have longer or shorter wavelengths than those of visible light.

Prisms and Rainbows

When white light passes through a special piece of glass called a prism, the light bends. Waves of different wavelengths bend by different amounts. The longest wavelengths bend the least. The shortest wavelengths bend the most. This bending separates the light waves so each color can be seen.

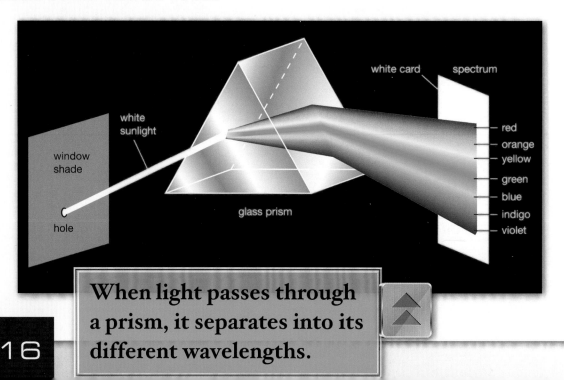

When light passes through a prism, it separates into its different wavelengths.

Prisms are found in binoculars, microscopes, and other instruments. Scientific instruments called spectroscopes use special prisms to separate light into a very wide spectrum of colors. This allows scientists to study the light from distant stars and other bodies in space.

Drops of water can also act as prisms. When light waves pass through raindrops, the light waves separate. This happens because the raindrops bend the light waves just as a prism does. The separated light waves appear as a rainbow, or a multicolored arc, in the sky.

COMPARE AND CONTRAST

How are raindrops like prisms? How are they different?

Sunlight separates into its different wavelengths of color as it passes through raindrops.

Light and Sight

An object can be seen only if light travels from the object to an eye that can sense it. Light can travel to an eye when an object gives off light or when an object reflects, or bounces back, light.

People see the sun because it gives off its own light. But people see the moon because light from the sun reflects off of it.

At night, the moon is illuminated by the sun. Although

Sunlight contains harmful radiation that can damage your eyes.

> During the waning crescent phase, the moon becomes less and less visible.

we do not see the sun at night, it is still shining from behind our planet. The moon and Earth are constantly moving, so light from the sun hits the moon and bounces toward Earth

THINK ABOUT IT

Why do we see stars in the night sky?

in different ways every day. As a result, a person standing on Earth sees different views of the moon at different times. These varying appearances are called phases.

How Much Light Gets Through?

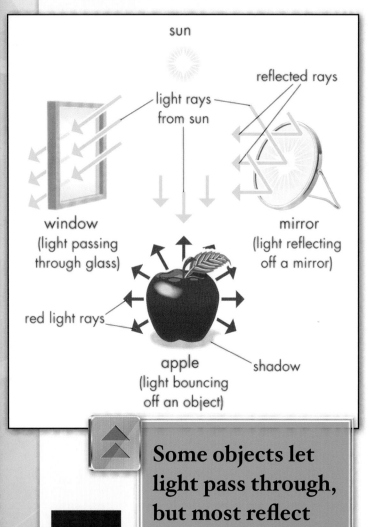

sun

light rays from sun

reflected rays

window
(light passing through glass)

mirror
(light reflecting off a mirror)

red light rays

apple
(light bouncing off an object)

shadow

Some objects let light pass through, but most reflect all or some light.

When only the surface of an object (such as the moon) can be seen, the object is said to be opaque. Opaque objects do not let light pass through them. Instead, they reflect and absorb light. As a result, they are not see-through. A mirror is an example of an opaque object that reflects almost all of the light that hits it.

A colored object reflects only certain

Most windows are transparent, making them easy to look through.

wavelengths of light. The reflected light is the color the object appears to be. For example, a red apple absorbs all the colors of light that hit it except for red light.

Materials that do not absorb or reflect much light are transparent, or see-through. Clear glass is transparent because most of the light that hits it passes through it. Objects that allow some, but not all, light to pass through them are called translucent. Stained-glass windows are translucent.

COMPARE AND CONTRAST

How do opaque and transparent objects differ? How are they similar?

ANIMALS AND VISIBLE LIGHT

Humans depend on sight to do many things. During the day, sunlight lights the world and makes it possible for us to see. At night, we are unable to see unless we produce our own light.

Humans see light in what is called the visible range, which includes all colors of light seen in a rainbow.

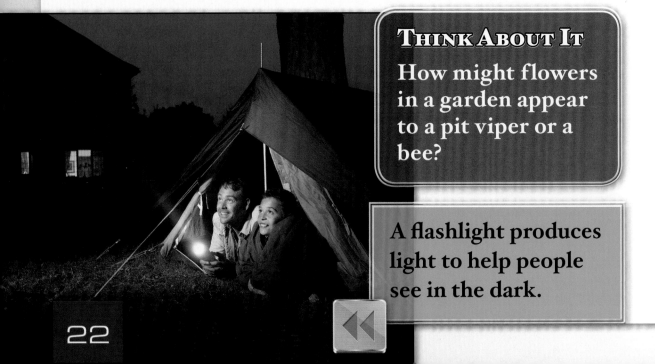

THINK ABOUT IT

How might flowers in a garden appear to a pit viper or a bee?

A flashlight produces light to help people see in the dark.

A pit viper has a heat-sensitive pit between each eye and nostril.

Other animals see or sense different kinds of light.

Snakes called pit vipers, for example, have sense organs (called pits) that "see" rays that humans feel as heat. These rays are called infrared radiation. These pits help them sense heat coming from the body of their prey. Once a pit viper senses the heat, it can attack its prey even in the dark. Bees see some of the colors that humans see, but they are also sensitive to ultraviolet radiation. Ultraviolet radiation is beyond the range visible to humans.

LIGHT AND PLANTS

Light is necessary for life on Earth. Without it, there would be no green plants, and without plants there would be no animals. Through a process called photosynthesis, plants use sunlight to make their own food. Photosynthesis requires sunlight, chlorophyll, water, and **carbon dioxide**.

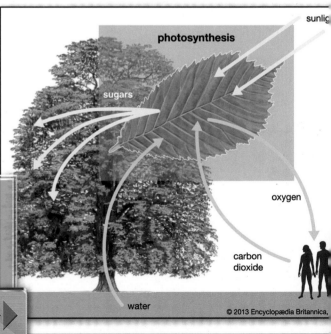

photosynthesis

sunlig

sugars

oxygen

carbon dioxide

water

© 2013 Encyclopædia Britannica,

Plants need sunlight to produce their own food through a process called photosynthesis.

Chlorophyll is a substance in all plants, especially in the leaves. Plants take in water from the soil and carbon dioxide from the air.

Photosynthesis starts when chlorophyll absorbs energy from sunlight. Green plants use this light energy to change water and carbon dioxide into oxygen and nutrients called sugars. The plants use some of the sugars and store the rest. The oxygen is released into the air.

People and other animals need oxygen to breathe to stay alive. They also rely on plants for food. They gain energy from the chemical energy that is stored in the sugars made during photosynthesis.

Animals get chemical energy by eating plants, or by eating other animals.

What Is Solar Energy?

Solar energy is light, heat, and other forms of energy given off by the sun. It fuels both plants and animals. Solar energy is the source of light for photosynthesis. It is also the source of heat that plants and animals need to survive. The heat from the sun causes water on Earth's surface to evaporate and form clouds that eventually provide fresh rainwater.

Heat from the sun causes water to evaporate into clouds. The clouds later provide rainwater.

These solar panels tilt to better absorb the energy from the sun as it moves across the sky.

Energy from the sun can also be collected and used to heat buildings and to make electricity. Most solar heating systems capture solar energy with a device called a flat-plate collector. The collector is a large plate of black metal covered with a sheet of glass. It is usually placed on the roof of a building. The plate absorbs sunlight and uses it to heat air or water that flows through pipes behind it.

THINK ABOUT IT

What different uses might there be for solar energy?

USING SOLAR ENERGY

There are other ways to use solar energy. A solar furnace uses the sun's heat by focusing light with mirrors to heat a small area. The heat is used to make steam. The steam can be used to make electricity in a power plant. Solar cells use the sun's light, turning it into electricity. A single solar cell makes only a little electricity, but groups of solar cells can provide electricity for whole buildings. Large groups of solar cells are called solar panels. Solar cells are also used in such products as calculators and watches.

Solar cells provide the power needed for this calculator.

Solar energy has two big benefits over fossil fuels like coal, oil, and natural gas. First, fossil fuels can be used up, but there is an endless supply of sunlight. Second, solar energy does not cause pollution, like burning fossil fuels does.

COMPARE AND CONTRAST

How are fossil fuels and solar energy different? How are they the same?

GLOSSARY

atom The smallest particle of an element that has the properties of the element and can exist either alone or in combination.

chemical reaction A chemical change that occurs when one or more substances combine to form a new substance.

electromagnetic radiation Energy in the form of electromagnetic waves, such as visible light, X-rays, and radio waves, that comes from the motion of charged particles in atoms.

electron A very small elementary particle within an atom that has a negative charge of electricity and travels around the nucleus of an atom.

evaporate To change into a gas.

fossil fuel A fuel, such as coal, oil, or natural gas, formed in the ground from plant or animal remains.

infrared Relating to rays like light but lying outside the visible spectrum at its red end.

nucleus The center of an atom.

oxygen One of the main elements that make up air and that is necessary for the survival of all plants and animals.

particle One of the very small parts of matter (as a molecule, atom, or electron).

photon A tiny bit or bundle of electromagnetic radiation.

prism A transparent object that usually has three sides and bends light so that it breaks up into rainbow colors.

solar cell A photoelectric cell that converts sunlight into electrical energy and is used as a power source.

ultraviolet radiation A kind of electromagnetic radiation having a wavelength shorter than that of visible light but longer than that of X-rays.

wavelength The distance from the peak of one wave to the peak of another one.

X-ray A kind of electromagnetic radiation of a very short wavelength that can move through objects and act on photographic film as light does.

FOR MORE INFORMATION

Books

Johnson, Robin. *What Are Light Waves?* (Light & Sound Waves Close-Up). New York, NY: Crabtree Publishing, 2014.

Navarro, Paula, and Ángels Jiménez. *Magical Experiments with Light & Color* (Magic Science). Hauppauge, NY: Barron's Educational Series, 2014.

Pfeffer, Wendy. *Light Is All Around Us* (Let's-Read-and-Find-Out Science). Rev. ed. New York, NY: HarperCollins, 2015.

Riley, Peter D. *Light* (Moving Up with Science). New York, NY: PowerKids Press, 2017.

Royston, Angela. *All About Light* (All About Science). Chicago, IL: Heinemann Raintree, 2016.

Websites

Because of the changing nature of internet links, Rosen Publishing has developed an online list of websites related to the subject of this book. This site is updated regularly. Please use this link to access the list:

http://www.rosenlinks.com/LFO/light

INDEX